How to Be a Good Mom
(Or at Least Not an Epic Failure)

Steph Williams

Published by Purposeful Words Publishing,
www.purposefulwordspublishing.com.

Copyright © 2017 by Steph Williams. www.stephhwilliams.com.

Cover Illustration Copyright © Purposeful Words Publishing
Cover design by Tanner Cangelosi

To the stars of my show

(and my heart)

Contents

For you created me my inmost being;
you knit me together in my mother's womb.
I praise you because I am fearfully and wonderfully made;
your works are wonderful, I know that full well.
My frame was not hidden from you
when I was made in the secret place.
When I was woven together in the depths of the earth,
your eyes saw my unformed body.
All the days ordained for me were written in your book
before one of them came to be.
-Psalms 139:13-16 (NIV)

Introduction

Despite all our balking at generalizations and stereotypes, we, as a society, tend to gravitate toward labels and categories. We're always trying to peg and name – people, habits, personality traits, etc. And it's never more prevalent than when it comes to parenting and motherhood.

Movies, TV, and books typically portray mothers as one of two extremes: either the picture perfect June Cleaver-ish mom who bakes cookies every day with never a hair out of place; or the "I don't know where that brat is" mom who's more concerned with herself and/or her next fix (of whatever the vice is) to care about child-rearing. There are only a few examples in entertainment that don't fit these extremes – the ones that are an honest mixture of the two, a parent just trying to survive, think along the lines of "Malcolm in the Middle" or "The Middle" – and those are typically used as caricatures (i.e., for comedic value).

Likewise, we pigeon-hole parenting styles. A few years back, helicopter parenting versus free-range parenting articles were all the rage. Helicopter parents were the ones who might be considered overbearing and/or overprotective, always hovering around their kids. Free-range parents, on the other hand, were ones who let their kids fall down, make mistakes, get hurt. Though some took sides, the idea was that neither was necessarily a better way of parenting, but simply a way of evaluating your priorities in the role.

Perhaps it's the non-conformist in me, but I think most parents – most mothers – can't be labeled or categorized. Most of us are just making it up as we go along, willing to shift strategies, change tactics, and/or try to move mountains to find what works to best parent our children. Or to at least keep from killing them (or ourselves).

The funny thing is that the best way to parent our children is to simply be the best we can be for each of them, remembering that each is a unique creation specially molded by the God of the universe. As are you. You, mom (or dad), are a unique creation specially molded by the God of the universe. He knit you together in your mother's womb. Think on that for a moment. Think of the special care and infinite attention that takes.

That same God of the universe made you your child's parent (whether biological or otherwise). You and your children, each and every unique one, were literally made for each other. My husband, Bryan, and I have a 16-year-old, a 14-year-old and a 10-year-old, and, the truth is, they couldn't be more different.

The Girl (age 16):

Of course, children change every day. Despite the fact that we learn to eat, walk, talk, and attend to our own bodily functions within the first few years of life, I'm convinced that the most dramatic changes occur in our teens and early 20s; that's when we really become who we are going to be. When the Girl was about 10, I described her as "our ultra-girly, uber-sensitive and undoubtedly lovable little girl who thinks she's the third adult (and perhaps second in charge) in the family." I nicknamed her the Girl because I regularly called her "such a girl" in normal conversation. Now, she's traded in her princess dresses for the comfort of untucked, fandom t-shirts and jeans (she's more like me in this respect than either of us admit on most days). She's still more sensitive than most but is more guarded and doesn't wear her heart on her sleeve as much. And though she's no longer a "little girl" (she's taller than me now), she's just as lovable, caring more about the feelings of others than her own (except on her "moody teenager" days), and loves her family (even, and likely especially, her brothers) above most anything else (except perhaps the latest Netflix binge).

The Professor (age 14):

When the Professor was about 8, I described him as "our precocious middle child who, I'm fairly convinced, is fairly convinced he's the smartest member of this family." I nicknamed him Boy Genius at first because, even at a young age, he seemed to really thirst for knowledge, absorbed facts like water to a sponge and had a memory like an elephant. As he got older, his ability to spout off information, whether requested or unwanted, only strengthened, so his nickname "grew up" to

Professor. Who knows if he's technically a "genius," but some conversations with him are precursors to either genius or madness (I hear there's a fine line; one he says he's dancing across). He's always concerned with equal rights and standing up for anyone he perceives to be oppressed (except when he's oppressing his little brother). While he probably still thinks he's smarter than everyone else, dad and I are trying to teach the more necessary humility and people skills (well, mostly dad, since he's better at both than me). He loves one on one time with us, considers his sister one of his best friends and tolerates his little brother more (just barely) now that they don't share a room.

Wonder Boy (age 10):

Wonder Boy is the baby of the family; a fact he still uses to his benefit daily. He's kind, funny and a lot like the Energizer Bunny. I nicknamed him Wonder Boy because, as a toddler, he was obsessed with Underdog and regularly proclaimed himself a superhero. Years later, though he still loves superheroes (we all do), his obsession now is with friends. He's barely off the bus in the afternoons before he's asking to go to a friend's house or have a friend over. He's the most outgoing member of the family and is always the life of any party. The name Wonder Boy still fits because I regularly wonder what the heck he's thinking, how he can have so much energy ALL.THE.TIME, and/or if he'll be the death of me. One thing's for sure, with his big heart for people, he's most certainly wonderfully made.

This Book:

Despite the presence of "how to" in the title, this is not a self-help book. I have no expert child-rearing credentials or special qualifications apart from being a mom of three. I've been blogging about life with kids, sometimes more consistently than others, since the oldest was 7. It's been a way for me to treasure the good moments and hopefully learn from the bad ones. In January 2009, I had to take a check to Wonder Boy's new "preschool" to reserve his spot. As we were pulling out of the parking lot, I announced that Wonder Boy was going to start school on Friday. Though the Professor simply screamed "NOOOOO" (reminiscent of young Skywalker's response to Darth Vader's "Luke, I am your father," or at least of Buzz Lightyear's impression in *Toy Story 2*), the Girl was perplexed.

"Why does he need to go to school," she asked, "what will you be doing?" I explained that I would be teaching a class or two at a local university and needed Wonder Boy to go to school while I was teaching. The Professor's shocked "You're a teacher?!" was again overshadowed by the Girl's inquisition (notice the difference in how their synapses fire?). She asked, "What are you going to teach, like history or a normal class?" Resolving that I couldn't possibly wrap my head around why "history" and "normal" classes are exclusive of one another, I answered, "I'm going to teach about writing." Then, there was silence.

Now, please understand, silence has always been a precious commodity in the car; our children are talkers. I thought, either they were contemplating what I'd said or had been sidetracked by whatever was in the DVD player (psh, no-brainer, right?). So I turned the volume up on the radio, assuming the conversation was indeed over.

Then I heard the Girl and Professor talking, apparently to each other, and I adjusted the radio just enough so that I could hear what they were saying. I'm guessing that maybe he asked her something about my teaching because I heard:

Girl: *Well, she's really good at writing and … fixing problems and … being a mommy and … answering questions …*

Professor: *Yeah, she could teach a "how to be a good mommy" class!*

Wow. Granted, I'm pretty sure he's (to this day) a momma's boy, but aw shucks. I'm still not sure whether they knew I was listening or that they would have remembered had I not blogged about it, but I can guarantee it's not something I'll ever forget.

I don't share that story to brag or even pretend that I'm an authority on the subject. To the clarity of a child, "being a mommy" ranks right up there with fixing problems and answering questions – which, let's face it, is pretty much in the job description. So, what follows is not meant to be the be-all, end-all story of parenting, but rather my take on what I've learned (and written down) over the last near decade. In my humble opinion, there are five "rules" of parenting:

Rule #1: Don't beat yourself up (even when you're certain you deserve it).

Rule #2: Laugh a little (or a lot) (and especially at yourself).

Rule #3: Listen to everything (and hold onto the good stuff).

Rule #4: Love (even when you don't like).

Rule #5: Give it (all) to God.

I certainly don't think I'm the best mom in the world or even that my motherhood experiences are all that unique. I simply wanted to put this book together to provide some hopefully entertaining anecdotes full of learning and encouragement without arrogance (or even a sense that I have it all figured out).

Oh, and lots of parentheticals (if you haven't already noticed).

Unless the Lord had given me help,
  I would soon have dwelt in the silence of death.
When I said, "My foot is slipping,"
  your love, O Lord, supported me.
When anxiety was great within me,
  your consolation brought joy to my soul.
-Psalms 94: 17-19 (NIV)

Rule #1: Don't Beat Yourself Up
(Even When You're Certain You Deserve It)

Show of hands: how many moms and dads out there have felt like failures at one point or another? If you didn't raise your hand, you're lying … to yourself or the world. The cold hard truth is that every parent everywhere has at some point felt the sting of failure. Let's say, for example, that something negative happens to our kids that's really our fault. That negative could be something we view as huge or something that, in the grand scheme of things, really isn't that big of a deal. But, no matter the size of the problem, if we've created it, we feel shame and guilt. Or let's say we react poorly to a situation with them or in front of them, and then we beat ourselves up for the poor reaction. Or maybe we just simply second guess our every decision, certain that we don't know what we're doing as parents.

I can't tell you how many times I've made my kids late. One recent morning, when we arrived early to the kids' weekly church group, the Girl exclaimed, "Are we early?! That NEVER happens!" Much of parenting is acting as a glorified taxi driver (though I'm not sure where the glory is in stale cheerios or smelly feet). Several years back, I got the Professor to school 15 minutes late … on the first day. There was no question that his being late was

9

my fault. Even though I'd said we weren't leaving the house until 7:30 a.m., both big kids were completely ready (including shoes, which is often a subject of debate) and had eaten breakfast before 7. But I had a plan: take the Girl, who was starting her first year of middle school, first, and then the boys, who were beginning 3rd grade and pre-K in the same building, since I'd have to park and walk in with Wonder Boy. When we got to the Girl's middle school, I was met with a drop-off line that extended out of the parking lot and onto the road for at least a mile. (School drop-off/pick-up lines are my Kryptonite). By the time we arrived at the Professor's elementary, school had been in session for 15 minutes. He was clearly upset, not wanting to walk into a new class late and have everyone stare at him. I kept saying it was no big deal since the school didn't issue tardies during the first week, but, inside, I felt terrible.

Now, that day was probably not the first time I'd made one or more of the children late to something, and it certainly was not the last (just ask the Girl, who regularly has to apologize for me at her babysitting jobs), but it is the reason they've been bus-riders ever since; and I do believe kids are more resilient than we sometimes give them credit. But I knew what the Professor was anticipating – walking into a new classroom, with a new teacher who has to stop talking to the class to acknowledge the late kid, while every eye in the place finds that kid's colorless face – and the anticipation created a hollow feeling in his stomach. My actions had created that hollow feeling. On the first day of school. Watching him walking away from me down that hallway, I had one sarcastic, negative, self-bashing thought: "I am #motheroftheyear!"

I think it's pretty safe to say that we've all been there. And in the era of social media – with everyone sharing their best moments on Facebook, their super-mom creations on Pinterest, and in-your-face mom blogs – it's pretty easy to feel less than as parents, like we're not quite good enough. Don't get me wrong: I like social media. As I hate talking on the phone, the different social media apps allow me to stay in touch with friends and family. I certainly would rather people post the best parts, rather than their worst. And I'm a huge fan of the Internet in general; a wealth of information at our fingertips (just remember not to believe everything you read on the web). The problem is one of comparison. We spend so much time now looking into the virtual windows of others' lives and, whether we mean to or not, we compare ourselves to what we see and read. Whether it's the sarcastic #motheroftheyear or the overly organized family on Pinterest, we make judgments about the posters and our "lesser" selves.

I used to be organized. No, really, I think it was something I was known for. I was even a bit of a neat freak. Everything had a place and was in its place (or else Steph turned into the Hulk). I kept a meticulous calendar and kicked the proverbial butts of to-do lists. Key words: "used to," as in, past tense. And then I had kids. Okay, it wasn't really that quick of a change, like overnight or the flipping of a switch. But there was a fundamental shift in how I approached management of the family when I stopped working full-time and became what I never thought I'd call myself: a stay-at-home mom.

Back in 2006, I took an approximate 3-year sabbatical from practice (and then quit being a lawyer for good in 2010). I'm not sure if I thought I wouldn't have

11

to juggle as much without the career (boy, was I wrong!) or if I just became more forgetful (or more tired). Between 2006 and 2009, we moved three times to three different states. Some days I feel as though I've forgotten more than I ever knew, and now, if I don't write it down, it ain't happening. This goes for buying grocery items, putting events on the calendar, or simply remembering to tell dad something when he gets home. My lack of organization and/or forgetfulness has been the source of some good old-fashioned "beating myself up."

The Professor has been on medication for high cholesterol since he was 7 years old. We discovered that his lousy cholesterol (LDL) was higher than the average bear's when he was about 2. A few years before that, his Pepa (Bryan's dad), who I'd always thought was perfectly healthy, had been abruptly hospitalized with several blocked arteries. Of course, it turned out to be a cholesterol issue and one that is genetic for the Williams' men. So when Pepa gave us all a fright, Bryan's doctor suggested he get tested as well, and his LDL was through the roof. When it couldn't be controlled with diet (that's a whole other story in itself), he began taking cholesterol-lowering medication. Our awesome pediatrician at the time recommended we start monitoring the Professor's and, at age 2, his LDL was 182. For years, we simply continued to monitor his numbers (and limit his French fries). When you move states three times in as many years, simple monitoring can get complicated. You've got to get established with a pediatrician who then refers you to a specialist who then runs tests (draws blood after fasting) … yada, yada, yada. By the time we moved to Arkansas in 2009, the Professor was overdue for a lipid check, and we had to jump through all the hoops again. We finally got an appointment scheduled with the Arkansas Children's

Hospital Endocrinology Clinic … for six months out! I put the appointment on the calendar, and we waited. And waited some more. In the meantime, life happened. When the morning of the appointment was finally upon us, the Professor (missing a day of school) and I made the hour-long trek to Little Rock, got checked in at the clinic, and then I realized I forgot to have him fast. I'm no doctor, but apparently you can't get an accurate cholesterol reading from bloodwork unless you've been fasting. Yet another example of momma dropping the ball. So at this long-awaited and essentially wasted appointment, we had to schedule another, another missed day of school when I could get him back on an empty stomach. From then on, the appointments (which are roughly every six months to a year now) are not simply jotted on the calendar; they all include "FASTING" in bold and color, with at least two reminders for the day before. Because if it doesn't get written down … hey, at least I learn from my mistakes sometimes, right?

Sometimes.

Sometimes I learn. Sometimes I make the same mistake over and over again. And then beat myself up for it. But what good does the beating myself up do? It just makes me feel like a failure … or like I want to crawl in a hole and never come out. But that's not living. And it's not parenting either.

This happened to me again (for the eleventy-millionth time) just the other day. We were pit-stopping at McDonald's on a day trip to Little Rock when I acted more like a child than anyone else in the car. As the worker outstretched her arms to hand me the full drink carrier, I withdrew my hands as though burned and said, "Oh, we don't need that." When she said she was required to use it, I reluctantly took it, quickly removing the drinks so that I could give the tray back to her before our food arrived. I held the tray out of my car window for several minutes before she opened the drive-thru window to say she wasn't allowed to take anything back from me. I scoffed, "Really?" and when she nodded, dropped it out of my window to the ground. Yes, I littered. In that moment, I was frustrated with the attitude I perceived from her and the ridiculousness of the situation, and I behaved like a child. And my children saw the whole thing. As we pulled back onto the road, I was immensely embarrassed and wishing I could take the last several minutes of my life back. Thinking about all the times in their lives I wished I could have a do-over, I quietly said to my daughter, "I shouldn't have done that." Saying nothing but nodding in agreement, she understood, I'm certain, what I was feeling. Children understand that we all make mistakes, whether we want to admit it or not. I'd already messed up. All I could do at that point was show how sorry I was and try my best to do better next time. Because there will always be a "next time," another chance to make a mistake.

Becoming a mother changes everything … your priorities, your perspective, your hopes and fears, your body, your ability to pee in private …. And that last one is important (other than for obvious reasons) because suddenly you never go anywhere alone. Now, there might be those few and far between moments when you steal away to the grocery store, leaving your little ones with daddy, or when they are at school and/or childcare while you work. For the most part, though, what seems like more often than not is that despite having already given birth you have an appendage that is child. That child (or children) is always there, always watching, always listening, and always learning. Nevertheless, I'm a firm believer that everyone needs "me" time (which is why I stay up until the wee hours of the morning because it's quiet or retreat to my room for "a nap" every chance I get).

In March 2013, I was lucky enough to go the ultimate of all girls' trips: two friends and I hopped the pond to partake in the Harry Potter Studio Tour. While I was out gallivanting in London, Bryan took the kids on a day trip to Petit Jean State Park. During one of our phone check-ins, he shared a "quotable moment" from the Professor. They'd been hiking all day and even trekked down a "treacherous" trail to stand behind the waterfall as all the other trekkers were on the trail side – the safe side – likely pointing at my husband, #fatheroftheyear. (At this point in the retelling, Bryan paused to interject: "I'm sure they were all commenting on what a bad parent I am, because no one else was back there.") Afterward, the Girl said "That was so cool. I couldn't think about my past or my future, just about what was happening right then." To which the Professor replied, with a big smile, "You know what that's called? A moment of awesomeness. I have them all the time."

Quotable indeed, and true to form. I, of course, shared this with my fellow London gallivanters, as I so often do with Professor stories. At dinner out with the family a few days later, I was sharing how my friends always get a kick out of those stories. This was when Wonder Boy spoke up: "I know you wish I wasn't your son." Stunned silence all around. Finally finding my voice, I said, "What do you mean?! Of course I want you for my son." When he didn't reply, the Professor interjected, "Well, cause you're always offering to give him away."

Looking from brother to brother, I saw the younger nod his downturned head.

And it's true, I would often reply to "he's so cute!" comments with "you want him?" or the like. Trying to be funny, all in good humor, of course. But it's not funny if no one's laughing. Looking at his sad face thinking I don't want him just broke my heart. You know what that's called? A moment of epic failure. And unfortunately, I have them all the time.

So I vowed to him then and there that I'd never say it again, and spent the rest of the night trying to convince him how much I love him and kicking myself for being a moron. Little eyes and ears see and hear everything, and their owners may not think about what happened before or what is to come, just how they feel in the moment. Though words can't break bones, they can hurt deeply; and we all must watch our words to make our moments awesome.

Yet again, I had to admit I made a mistake. I hate having to do that. Everyone does. But I can't promise I won't make mistakes, act inappropriately, say something wrong, or hurt feelings, etc. And neither can you. And here's the golden nugget: I don't think our kids want us to make that promise. Because they're going to make mistakes, act inappropriately, say something wrong, hurt feelings, and the list goes on and on. All we can do is show them the right way to be after – admission of fault, sincere remorse, and … trying.

As David said in Psalms 94 (NIV):

When I said, "My foot is slipping,"

your love, O Lord, supported me.

Rather than beating ourselves up, feeling like epic failures or #motheroftheyear, we've got to jump right back in. If you spend time dwelling on how you've erred, you'll miss all the good parts. So, just as we're always telling our kids: dust yourself off and get back on the bike, we must acknowledge our mistakes and move on. Reacting the right way in a bad situation isn't easy. It's like those first few pushes when the training wheels come off. You feel off-kilter and a little like the ground is moving beneath you. But you keep pushing and gain your balance.

Being good when it's hard requires effort. But the best lesson we can teach our children is that it's worth trying. We can let our kids watch us as we try our best to be better people.

STEPH WILLIAMS

A cheerful heart is good medicine,
    but a crushed spirit dries up the bones.
-Proverbs 17:22 (NIV)

RULE #2: Laugh a Little (or a Lot)
(And Especially at Yourself)

As our children age, we progress through different stages of parenting. These stages, unfortunately much like the labels or categories I complained of earlier, follow our child's growth: we're parents of infants, parents of toddlers, parents of small children, parents of teenagers, parents of young adults. The thing all of those categories have in common: parents who are figuring things out as they go along.

One thing parents of small children often learn the hard way is how much of the public your kids can handle (and vice versa). Back when the kids ranged from two to nine years old, dining out with the pack was an infrequent treat. We had pretty much limited our dining out escapades to family-friendly eateries since the Girl's 15-month-old tantrum antics nearly brought down the house and got us banned for life from an upscale Birmingham-area restaurant. Memories of her red-faced screams and the disparaging looks from other diners, coupled with a 2-year-old Wonder Boy's tendency for decorating the floor (and, a few times, any neighboring diners!) with our choice of sustenance (potentially half-chewed first) often made us think very carefully about partaking anywhere other than home. Plus, eating out with the children often grated on my nerves. I felt like I spent the majority of every meal saying things like, "sit still," "wipe your face … No! Use a napkin," "Sit up right," "Leave your [sister/brother/foot] alone," "Stop swinging your feet," "Close your mouth when you chew," and "Eat!" I wonder now how much my constant "parenting" bothered other patrons more than the silliness of my kids. Seriously, it's a wonder I had time to eat (maybe that's why I was so skinny then). And most of what I was yammering on about was silliness, just kids being kids.

So I became an over-sharer of pictures of messy-faced kids; determining that until (if ever) my kids learned some manners, I'd just keep my camera phone handy. (I've got some great shots, like the Girl with rib meat dangling from her teeth, the Professor smiling proudly despite the sauce circling his lips and dripping down his arm, and Wonder Boy drinking refried beans through a straw, that will make for prime graduation/wedding flashbacks). Now that they're older, I've less to "correct" at meal time (which is probably why I've gained weight), but our dinners together are still just as silly. And there's always someone with food on his/her face; sometimes it's me.

While family meal time is a good source of silliness (and blackmail photos), car rides are where we thrive. We, as a society, spend so much time in the car … traveling to and from work, school, church, practice, games, lessons, friends' houses, etc. When our children were younger, I'd imagine the driver's seat encapsulated by a cone of silence, free from the sounds of whining or fighting amongst siblings. My imagination is pretty good but never strong enough. Inevitably, the noise would seep in (and require I get involved as mediator, peacemaker and sometimes sovereign dictator or benevolent overlord). Looking back, I'm thankful that I couldn't "tune out" the backseat. Some of the funniest (or craziest) conversations have occurred on the open road.

Last year, we traded in the family van for a shiny new SUV. The family van, which we affectionately called "Aunt Bee," joined the family when our youngest was about 6 months old. Even still, the older two barely remember the family vehicle before her. We'd had her for 8 years and she was pushing 200 thousand miles when we finally let her go. Indiana Jones said, "It's not the years, it's the mileage." Well, where Aunt Bee was concerned, it wasn't the years or the mileage, but the … experiences. You see, Aunt Bee was not only there for the raising of three children; she also survived at least 6 moves, countless road trips (with and without dogs), carpools with friends, and a wide variety of live and inanimate cargo – from instruments to sports equipment to furniture to household pets to farm animals. Over the years, Aunt Bee toted humans, dogs, birds, lizards, snakes, spiders, mice, dairy goats, chickens, rabbits … But it wasn't just what she'd carried; it was what she'd "seen." There was a "conversation mirror" on the outside of the sunglasses holder, just above the rearview mirror. It was a surprisingly nice little feature (and one I'm missing in the SUV, allowing me to truly have eyes in the back of my head (something all mothers need at times). Once the Girl said we should install a wide-view camera to capture all the conversations and happenings that took place in the van. She was probably on to something. Take, for instance, this … er, um … teaching moment from a few years ago:

As the song "Pour Some Sugar On Me" started playing on the radio …

Dad (in passenger seat): (Turning the volume up slightly and turning to face the kids) *This band, Def Leppard, was very big when your mom and I were younger. Then, the drummer was in a car wreck and lost one of his arms. After a while, the band came back and the drummer played with just one arm.*

Me (driving, and thus, facing forward): *Just as good as before.*

Dad: (To Mom) *Well, very good still.* (Then, to kids) *So, you see why we get very aggravated when you say you can't do something. Look at what he did with just one arm … He's playing this song with one arm.*

A few moments of silence passed and then …

Professor: *What happened to his arm?*

At this point, dad and I exchanged exasperated looks because we were used to the boy not always paying attention.

Dad: *It was ripped off in the wreck …*

Professor (interjecting): *No, I know, but what happened to it? What'd they do with it? … I'd put it in a museum …*

As dad just laughed …

The Girl: *That's not the point.* (You could almost hear the sound of her eyes rolling).

While the conversation continues between the kids in the back …

Dad: (To me) *I think he's a genius.*

And it was my turn to laugh.

Dad: *No, really, his mind works differently than most people.*

Then from the back, we hear …

The Girl: *What if you could buy it?*

Professor: *I would SO buy it …*

Me: *NO SEVERED LIMBS IN YOUR ROOM!*

So I'm pretty sure that the point of the lesson was lost but at least they can't say I've never told them not to bring body parts home.

There once was a show called "Kids Say the Darndest Things." It's true, the title of the show, I mean. Kids really do say some wacky but often brutally honest things that spew out of their mouths without crossing their brains first, which I think might be the unofficial definition of "darndest." The sometimes refreshing and oftentimes inopportune honesty of a child is one of the things we're supposed to train them up right about as parents, I suppose. You never want to teach your kids to lie, but it's important to teach them about tactfulness, respect, and timing. I mean, just because honesty is the policy doesn't mean you have to be rude (I think I was an adult before I accepted this and it kills me to think how I used to speak to people; but we're past rule #1 so I'm letting it go). Sometimes kids really don't mean things to be rude or hurtful but, again, they just don't give the words much thought before those words come roaring out of their mouths.

23

A few years ago, I took the two oldest to the local bowling alley while little brother was still at daycare. They'd gotten some good-student coupons for free games during spring break. When we were leaving, the Girl said she wished we could play all day, which prompted the following discussion:

Me: *No way I could play all day. My arm already hurts.*

The Girl: *Your arm hurts? Why?*

Me: *I guess from lugging that ball. I don't know.*

The Girl: *My arm doesn't hurt.*

Professor: *Mine neither.*

Me: *Well, of course not. Y'all are young whippersnappers.*

Professor: (snickering) *"Whippersnappers"?*

Me: (ignoring the snicker) *Like I bet your legs didn't hurt at all when we were climbing that trail on Saturday, huh?*

Both: *Nope.*

Me: *See. 'Cause y'all are young and doing stuff doesn't hurt as much.*

The Girl: *So if you fall down and hurt your knee, it hurts worse than if I fall down and hurt my knee?*

Me: *No, not necessarily.*

The Girl: *So if I'd been older when I cracked open my head, it would've hurt more?*

(Side note: she didn't actually crack open her head; she got hit in the head by a tool that fell and got a maybe a half-inch cut on her scalp. But saying "cracked open my head" warrants more sympathy I suppose.)

Me: (sighing) *No, I'm pretty sure that hurts the same always.* (Pausing to choose my words more carefully) *I mean like your muscles hurt more when you're older. You're young and your muscles don't hurt as much as mine. 'Cause you're young whippersnappers.*

Professor: (snickering again) *"Whippersnappers."*

The Girl: *But if we're doing the same thing, why do your muscles hurt more?*

Me: (a little exasperated) *I don't know. I guess 'cause I'm old and cranky.*

The Girl: *You're not old. You're not old until you're like a hundred or something.*

Professor: *But you are cranky.*

The conversation continued between the two of them in the back seat, arguing whether I was crying or laughing up front. The Girl thought for sure that the Professor had hurt my feelings, but he just kept saying, "What? It's true."

And it probably is, at least sometimes. But, to be fair, the Professor's next words of wisdom had to do with choosing to give up a foot rather than the Internet because you could buy a solid gold replacement foot on the

Internet as long as you still had it. Again with the body parts. Good thing we covered that lesson.

Now I could say I don't know where he gets this stuff, but, the truth is, we all say crazy things. On family vacation about five years ago, in my state of sheer exhaustion from chasing kids in the sun, I may have said a few crazy things myself, like:

> *"Pee on yourself."*

> *"If I'd been a boy, I'd have ogled too."*

> *"Don't touch anyone's balls but your own."*

> *"I think parasailing would be fun."*

Okay, as it turns out, only the last one was actually crazy.

The Professor got stung by a jellyfish. I think he got stung multiple times all around the same spot on his foot. So as he ran-skipped back into the condo hollering about the pain, I said, "Pee on yourself." I honestly didn't know if peeing on jellyfish stings was a real solution or not; I just remembered the "Friends" episode where Monica gets stung and Joey is going to pee on it because that supposedly dulls the pain but he gets "stage fright" so Chandler has to do it. Yes, as my child writhed in pain, I was thinking about a TV show and looking for a laugh. For the record, he did it and said it helped; #motheroftheyear, yeah baby!

During one of the many pool excursions that week, we were tossing a ball back and forth. Bryan practically nailed the Professor in the head because he was busy looking elsewhere. The Professor, eight at the time mind you, was … preoccupied … by the rather tan, bikini-clad young woman who had stopped on the steps of the pool to hand-ladle water onto various parts of herself. Later, when we were picking on the Professor for getting busted, Bryan asked with a grin, "All I wanna know is, does the boy have good taste?" To which I answered, "If I'd been a boy, I'd have ogled too."

Taking a break from the sand and sun, we went to play mini-golf one night after dinner. Wonder Boy, four at the time, didn't quite get it. He liked swinging the club, at everything in sight, but even more he liked picking up all the balls after people hit them. After telling him several times, with no success, to leave them alone, I said rather loudly, "Don't touch anyone's balls but your own!" Prompting an embarrassed "Mom!" from the Girl.

At one point during the week, I saw some people parasailing and said, "I think parasailing would be fun." After a good fit of laughter at my initial statement, Bryan kept coming back to this statement all week. I don't like heights. I don't like falling. I don't like going underwater. Basically, I don't like not being in control. Clearly, that was the craziest thing I'd said all week.

And we all got a good laugh from it. I couldn't help but laugh at my own silliness. A cheerful heart, indeed.

Unfortunately, sometimes the things we say don't warrant laughter (or shouldn't). In wasn't until maybe five or six years ago that I became convicted about the type of language I regularly used. Basically, I used to curse like a sailor. Anytime I felt a twinge of guilt about using profanity, I'd make excuses like "They're just words; it's people that make them bad" or "It's commonplace in the environment I work in" or some other nonsense. I'd even let the really bad ones (you know which ones I'm talking about) fly free in the presence of my children. But ultimately I began to feel God working on me more and more about the words I chose to let loose from my lips. I, being the imperfect being that I am, still slip up on occasion, but it's less and less frequent.

When the Professor was seven, we literally washed his mouth out with soap. He'd spouted off a word he shouldn't have known much less use and we took drastic measures. The sad part was that he probably learned it from me. Once it was all said and done, Dad and I were in the kitchen, listening to the Professor brushing his teeth for the third time and spitting profusely into the sink. Quietly, Dad asked me, "We did the right thing, right?" and I just shrugged. Then, the Professor walked through the kitchen, mumbling something about still having the taste in his mouth, when Dad asked him, "So does [friend] say those kinds of words." The Professor, darting his eyes to me, simply responded with a "Yeah." I don't know for sure if it was the soap, but he never said it or anything like it in our presence again. In fact, any one of the kids will pretty quickly admonish me when I do let one slip. I suppose they're my accountability partners on that one.

Of course, I'd be remiss if I didn't share the rest of the story. Once the Professor and his soapy mouth was out of earshot, Dad turned to me with the hint of a smirk, "So are you going to call [friend]'s mom like …" and before he could finish, because I knew where he was going, I yelled, "No, I will not be Ralphie's mom!" Yes, in the middle of an important parenting moment, the two adults-in-charge were clearly only thinking of *A Christmas Story.*

What can I say? Laughter is good medicine.

Her children arise and call her blessed …
-Proverbs 31:28 (NIV)

RULE #3: Listen to Everything
(And Hold onto the Good Stuff)

Our children grow up so quickly. I can remember when mine were very little and people would tell me that, or say things like "cherish every moment" or "don't blink." Honestly, I'd be secretly rolling my eyes. In the thick of parenting small kids, whether one or several, it seems a bit like hanging on to a light pole in the middle of a lightning storm. So much of our existence is spent caring for ones who cannot care for themselves that we may neglect our own well-being. Then we reach points of breaking, of being frazzled messes whose grand accomplishment is surviving.

This is not to say that once children grow a little bit older, we're less likely to be frazzled messes. Often, in preparation for a new baby, especially the first, we spend a lot of time reading up on tips and strategies; but as our children age, we either don't have the time or the energy to do such "research" (that is, unless a specific, heavy problem arises). Honestly, though, it's not easier to parent one age over another (though it does help when they can feed themselves and/or use the bathroom without assistance). But it is true that no age is forever. If you're in the thick of a storm and thinking you may break, know that one day soon you'll be looking back on this moment rather than living it. So rather than beating yourself up (remember rule #1), really try to enjoy the ride. It'll be over before you know it.

The real truth to parenting is that we're raising these children to be adults, to be independent, to no longer need us (but to hopefully still like us). Just as we often judge ourselves against others or wonder what a friend or a complete stranger may think of our parenting, we too contemplate what our children think of us. I'm convinced that it's impossible to parent a child, perhaps particularly as mothers, without having the words, "I hate you" flung in your direction, spat from that beautiful mouth you helped to create. I suppose it's a part of life or goes with the territory. And even if we know, deep down, that those words weren't meant, that they were just a heated response to being denied something likely insignificant, they still sting. But we can't ignore these words, because we must listen to everything; you never know when you might hear something important.

My kids probably laughed out loud when they read that last sentence. They'll tell you one of my favorite sayings is "stop talking please." Sometimes, when frustration is running high, I drop the "please" and say the rest through gritted teeth. And it seems like a no-brainer that a parent should never tell a teenager to stop talking. Teenhood is a notoriously tight-lipped age, at least where parents are concerned. In my defense, though, my "stop talking please" is often in response to repeated requests for something I've already said no to or bickering between siblings. I hope I've never said it when one of them was trying to have a real conversation with me. I have somewhat of a reputation for saying what I think and being a bit no-nonsense. Just the other day, when I was sharing some sad news about a family member with the Professor and voiced my own uncertainty about telling him the details; he said, "No, I like that you're honest; you don't sugar coat."

The really awesome thing about listening to your kids is that you'll hear their love for you in the things they say to you and about you to others. When you're listening, you don't have to wonder what they think, or dwell on the words said in anger, because you'll have the affirmation you so desperately want from them. Those are the words to remember, to hold fast to; those are words of life.

Every so often, I get a glimpse of how my children see me. Sometimes the image is a positive one, and sometimes it's not. Of course, sometimes you've got to really look hard and/or cherry-pick to get to the good parts. Being the nerdy family we are, we often debate the really important issues like "What superpower would you want to have?" or "Who would win in a fight?" (hint: always Superman). A couple of years ago, we were determining which superhero each of us most closely fits (we often do this with TV and movie characters too; I said we were nerdy).

The Professor quickly assigned the Flash to Wonder Boy, because he has so much energy and never, ever slows down. The Girl was Kitty Pryde/Shadowcat, because she's sneaky (which seems negative but we didn't mean it's always a bad thing). It's just that sometimes, even when you'd think she was nowhere near you, somehow she'd know the details of a private conversation, like what someone was getting for Christmas. We all decided that the Professor was Cyborg, though he seemed disappointed that it didn't mean he'd talk like Arnold Schwarzenegger in *Terminator*. (He's still not happy with this selection). Cyborg definitely fit him though because he has excellent information recall (like scary good sometimes) and would regularly say things like, "I don't need a calculator; I have one in my head." Everyone seemed pretty satisfied that dad was Mr. Fantastic, without much explanation (perhaps because he wasn't present for the conversation to question it); but I'd guess it's because he holds us all together. Cyborg, I mean the Professor, said that I was Charles Xavier/Professor X, mainly because he said sometimes it seems like I can read his mind. Admittedly, I was proud of this one and didn't tell him that it's just mom experience, yo! But then he went on to say that no one really knows the extent of Xavier's power; like if he wanted to, he could get in someone's head and destroy them from the inside out. Huh? So my kid thinks I'm a mind-reader … and is maybe slightly afraid for his life. Talk about cherry-picking the positive. #motheroftheyear (my parenting might actually be working – talk about a moment of awesomeness!)

As if the hypothetical hero-turned-supervillain image isn't enough, my kids also expect me to be brutal in the event of an apocalypse. Continuing a conversation that started between Mema (Bryan's mom) and the kids, we were assigning jobs or roles for each family member in a post-apocalyptic world (hang in there, don't put down the book – trust me …). Because it's always good to plan ahead and because we don't have normal conversations in our family. Mema would be the cook. The Girl should be studying up on plants so she can be the resident herbologist. Everyone decided that the Professor needed to study up on alternative fuels but he rejected the appointment. He wanted to be the hunter or basically do anything with guns. Most everyone had donned me the executioner, with no pre-apocalyptic preparation required. Thanks, kids. They said I'd be the one to decide if you're an asset or a liability. If you're good for the community, you get to stay/live; if not, you're outta here. Just as I was starting to mentally question this view of me, the Professor began arguing once again about not liking his assigned job; to which I replied, "Dude, I'm gonna have to kill you." And just like that, question answered.

Sometimes the viewpoint is not something I would have ever expected. The kids often spend a week with Mema during the summer. One year, when we met at the halfway point between Arkansas and Alabama, we all decided to have lunch before sending the kids off for the week. Just as we were digging into our orders, Wonder Boy had to use the bathroom. Now, anyone who's ever gone anywhere with Wonder Boy knows that his bathroom trips are not brief. Bryan, having already gone in the bathroom to wash his hands when we arrived, had commented on the smell and was not too keen on returning for an extended visit. So he did what any self-respecting father would do, he tried to push it off on one of the older kids. He spent a good solid minute arguing with the Professor about who was going to escort Wonder Boy into the smelly bathroom before I stepped in with the voice of reason. As Bryan huffed and walked away with Wonder Boy, I rolled my eyes and jokingly asked Mema, "You sure you don't want all four kids this week?" To wit:

Professor: *Who's the fourth kid?*

Me: *Who do you think? Your dad.*

Professor: *I thought it might be you.*

Me: (scoffing) *Really? Who acts more like a kid — me or daddy?*

The Girl: *Well you're the one who gets all excited about Superman and comic books and movies.*

Professor: *And daddy's always saying no to stuff.*

Me: (surprised) *Daddy says "no" more than me?*

The Girl: *Yeah, he's always like, "No more soda." "No sugar."*

Professor: *Or "No butter."*

(In our defense, see the earlier discussion on cholesterol).

Me: *Wait, so you're saying I'm the fun parent?*

Both kids: *Yeah.*

Me: *But I'm always saying no or telling you to clean your rooms.*

The Girl: *Not really.*

Professor: *And butter is fun.*

(Clearly, the boy is deprived).

Me: (giddy) *Oh. My. Gosh. I need to record this. You have to tell your daddy I'm the fun parent. Let me bask in it.*

Neither, especially the Girl, was too happy about sharing this with daddy, but I couldn't let it go. You know, because we have to latch on to the good stuff. So when Bryan and Wonder Boy returned from the marathon bathroom trip, I said, in my giddy voice, "Guess who's the fun parent?!" Bryan was clearly taken aback at this revelation and exaggerated the hurt a little, at which point Mema stepped in to try to soothe his ego:

Dad: *Just because I don't let y'all eat a bunch of sugar ...* ["*Or butter,*" interjected the Professor; seriously you can't make this stuff up]. *Y'all think I'm not fun?*

Mema: *No, they're not saying that. Right, kids?*

Both kids nodded as I sat quietly, barely containing my glee.

Mema: *They're just saying momma's funner.*

Both kids: (in unison) *Funner's not a word.*

Professor: *Momma draws the line at grammar.*

A few high-fives across the table to let the kids know I was proud was met with a mumble from dad, "Well, I'm still not letting y'all eat sugar."

I would never have expected the kids to describe me as fun. I've always felt as though I spent the majority of my time telling them no and/or making them clean. But that's not what they perceive, and my knowing that gave me a little more confidence that they liked being around me. #Awesomeness.

That doesn't mean I'm all fun and games, though. And sometimes I am downright cranky (so Professor was definitely on to something) and yank the rug out from under everyone. Take, for instance, the time I pulled the plug on a camping trip ... in the middle of the night. One year for Spring Break, we had planned no trips or family activities because dad was really busy at work. But that Saturday morning before dawn, he got the bright idea that we'd go camp overnight at Petit Jean State Park. And I said "ok," because it sounded fun. The park was only about an hour's drive from home but by the time we packed for 3 kids, 2 dogs and us, and made a couple of stops for food and additional supplies, it was mid-day by the time we arrived at the campsite. We spent the afternoon walking trails and enjoying the scenery, then grilled out for dinner, made s'mores and roasted marshmallows. Then it was time for bed, and well you know that they say, all good things must come to an end.

I'd remarked earlier in the day that I felt more isolated and in touch with nature in our own backyard. I'd been saying for years that I wanted to spend a week alone in the woods. Like Thoreau. I wanted to go somewhere, be completely unplugged from the world with no deadlines, no worries … just for a little while. So as we were sitting there listening to the sounds of neighboring campers instead of crickets, I felt the need to tell everyone that this was not what I meant by being alone in the woods.

As pretty as the campsite is, it's been very commercialized. Within minutes of our arrival, the kids from one neighboring site were asking to pet our dogs and where we were from and a million more questions. Then one of the kids brought his puppy over on a flexi-lead to play with our dogs. The leash kept getting tangled on our dogs' tie-out. Then the kid kept telling me to hold back our lab so he wouldn't "be mean" to the puppy, and I was telepathically telling the lab to take the little sucker out (remember the Professor X comparison?). On the other side of us, there appeared to be one group stretch across multiple campsites with one main tailgating tent in the middle for the food … sort of like a compound.

We had set up two tents, the smaller for the kids behind ours, but with so many strangers around I didn't like the idea of not being able to see the kids. And then the temperature began to drop pretty quickly. So all five of us, well seven counting the dogs, piled into the larger tent. We divvied up the blankets and pillows that dad had packed, which were scarce, and tried to settle in. That proved a little more difficult than we'd expected because despite everyone being tired from our trail blaze, close quarters like that cause some intermittent giggling or arguing amongst the kids. And the compound neighbors didn't share our bedtime. Fortunately, we're a family of good sleepers, that is, everyone but me. It's a fact that if you get any one of them still for more than a minute, they'll be out; the boys, dad included, regularly doze in the car just on a quick trip to the grocery store. I, on the other hand, am not so lucky and regularly fight bouts of insomnia. So, despite the sounds of the compound - the laughter of adults, the few threats to children to "go to bed already" and the one presumed toddler who screamed "DADDY!" at the top of his lungs for a good solid five minutes – a slow steady rhythm of breathing developed in our tent. They'd all dozed off - the kids, Bryan, even the dogs. I lay there, switching from my eyes tight shut while on my side to lying on my back staring at the top of the tent, listening to the sounds next door and getting colder and colder. Bryan had packed three pillows (for five people), small "throw" blankets (not a single quilt), and one sleeping bag (which he admitted he'd planned for himself before I made him spread it out for the kids).

Finally, after about an hour, the neighbor's party died down and the voices began to fade away. I had several moments of quiet, lying there thinking if I could just ball my body up enough for the small blanket to cover me completely, I might make it through the night. That's when I heard it. The snoring. The snoring that wasn't coming from inside our tent. I watched each member of our tent in turn. No, this was a neighbor's snore. It proved too much for me. The fact that I was cold and that camping is supposed to be time "alone in the woods" and that I could hear some strange man snoring from a tent maybe ten feet away was just too much. I considered trying to sleep in the car but when I was leaving the tent, I noticed the kids balled up in fetal positions under their throw blankets. So I already couldn't sleep and was cold and was now worried that the kids were going to freeze to death. Knowing that I would not get a lick of sleep that night unless I took drastic measures, I made a decision.

I woke everyone up and told them ("loudly and 'yelly'" according to the Girl) we were going home. It was after midnight. I packed up the empty tent and the few remaining items we'd left outside; then we got the kids and dogs in the van (with the heat on full blast) while we dismantled the larger tent. I shone the flashlight around the campsite once more trying to ensure we hadn't left anything behind and we left. As we were driving away, Bryan said, "Wow, we must be expert campers if we can break down camp in the dark like that." I replied, "as long as we have all three kids and both dogs, anything else can be replaced." Then I put on the brake and looked in the back seat to confirm we'd done just that. Bryan told me later that while I was packing up the smaller tent, he'd asked the Girl if she was cold. She answered yes but that she could've waited until morning to leave. "You know, like a normal family would do," she said, "but we're not normal are we, Daddy?" To which he replied, "No, honey, we're not."

Despite the fact that I see myself as the disciplinarian, that I think I'm constantly using my outside voice with them or that I may spoil some of their fun, my kids give me a lot of grace. They forgive me when I mess up and they love me always. Just this morning, the Professor and I were talking about how frequently he calls me "awesome" (often when I know what he's talking about related to a game or some other kid thing he presumes parents don't know). At first, he denied it and tried to blame it on the pain meds he briefly took following his tonsillectomy. But I cited blog posts from way back as proof, because I always try to document the good. So he quietly said, "Wow, it must really make you feel good," and then, louder, "Okay, I'll keep saying it."

"Her children … call her blessed."

There's something really powerful about seeing yourself through the eyes of your children. And probably vice versa; so think about what they would see through your eyes.

...if I have a faith that can move mountains, but have not love, I am nothing.

...

Love is patient, love is kind. It does not envy, it does not boast, it is not proud. It is not rude, it is not self-seeking, it is not easily angered, it keeps no record of wrongs. Love does not delight in evil but rejoices with the truth. It always protects, always trusts, always hopes, always perseveres.
Love never fails.
--1 Corinthians 13:2, 4-8 (NIV)

RULE #4: Love
(Even When You Don't Like)

The older my children get, the more reflective (and sometimes scared) I become about the type of people I'm helping to mold. As most parents know, our children are not simply younger versions of ourselves. And just as there will be times that our children scream "I hate you" at us for some perceived injustice, it's just as likely that there will be times we don't like them all that much either. Now, I know that statement is a bit harsh, but it's nonetheless true. We've already established that our kids are no more perfect than we are. So they're going to make mistakes; they're going to do things we wish they wouldn't. But we can't, shouldn't, just walk away from them, turn our backs and say that's it.

Our children are blessings from God, even when they're little brats.

And sometimes we're the brats and just wish our children were mini-versions of the good parts of ourselves.

43

But part of growing up (at any age) is making mistakes, figuring out who you are, and forming (hopefully educated) opinions. Odds are, we're not going to agree with everything our kids say, do or think. But we're not called to agree with them; we're called to love them. (As an aside, wouldn't it be nice if we applied this to strangers as well?)

Over the years, the Girl and I have butted heads more than anyone else in the household. Perhaps it's because we're both female, or maybe we're more alike than either of us will typically admit. I used to wonder if I was harder on her than the boys simply because she's a girl (there's some psychology going on there above my pay grade). Contrary to public opinion on the matter, she and I are closer now that she's a teenager. The roughest years so far for us, I think, were about 8 to about 11; those were the years we had the hardest time communicating or even understanding each other.

At some point, I think, most mothers realize that their little darlings can either be sweet, angelic, "you'll always be my little girl" babies or the attitude sportin' "when did 8 become the new 13" pains in the you-know-whats. I wonder, though, how many see this in the span of less than a minute. When we first moved to Arkansas, and the kids had started a new school, they had been asking me regularly to eat lunch with them at school. I'd finally relented and planned to visit on the Friday before the Girl's 8th birthday, but that morning it seemed as if everything that could go wrong did. Just when I thought I'd had enough, the Girl came out of her room, still in her PJs despite our need to walk out the door, whining about not having anything to wear. I stomped to her closet, snatched a pair of pants and tossed them to the floor at her feet (looking back, I no longer question where she got her attitude). Whining continued, something about how she'd freeze to death in them when she sat down on the playground, and why hadn't I washed any of her jeans, and why don't I ever listen to her, and she didn't like those pants, and, in case I didn't hear her before, she'd "free-eeeze" to "deathhhh" in them. So I said, "Just get dressed so I can take you to school and not have to talk to you about your pants until you get home!" As she began to cry, she said, "But I thought you were coming to eat lunch with us." I was shocked. When I'm mad at someone, I certainly don't want to have lunch with them. I just assumed she'd want to be rid of me for awhile too. But not my Girl. Underneath any attitude, despite all the bickering and mean words, she still loved me and wanted me around.

Not-so-surprisingly, that was not our only disagreement about clothing. About the time the Girl entered middle school, there was a Disney Channel show called "Shake It Up." It focused on two tween best friends who get gigs as back up dancers on their favorite TV show. One of the friends, CeCe, had a style all her own, often wearing layers of clothing including tights or leggings, sporting rips and tears in jeans, and jacketing shirts that one wouldn't normally consider as outerwear. The Girl wanted to be CeCe. Seriously, she wanted to dance, talk and dress like her. I've never been considered a fashionista and surely have never been particularly in tune with what's hot or trending. But I wasn't sure that the Girl's imitation showed the same amount of style. She would often layer t-shirts and wear her farm boots with skirts and capris. Daily, I'd struggle with not making her change before school, doing my best to simply let her express herself. Then she came home from school one day and said that maybe she'd stop trying to copy CeCe so much. As I began to wonder if a classmate had said something mean, she explained that the counselor came to talk to the class about the importance of being yourself and not giving into peer pressure. She translated that to her copying CeCe. I was so preoccupied with my desire to make her change that it never occurred to me to turn the issue into a lesson on peer pressure. The way it turned out, she was allowed to learn and make a decision for herself without me pressuring her to be something she's not.

Sometimes reigning in the mom pressure is easier than other times. The first time the Girl decided to be a vegetarian was when she was 11. She was never a big meat-eater to begin with, so she and a couple of her friends had decided this while waiting in the lunch line at school (I'm not sure what this says about the lunch offering that day). Of course, by the time they'd gotten their trays to the lunch table, the Girl was the only one sticking to it. She researched the different types of vegetarian diets and talked to dad about the importance of still getting the nutrients she needs. For the first few weeks, I was perhaps not all that supportive. For someone like me, who believes the definition of a "good meal" is a medium rare filet mignon, this whole thing was odd. I kept offering her things she couldn't eat and regularly said "Give it to us raw – any wriggling!" in my best Gollum voice. But she never wavered. When I finally realized it was something important to her, I caved and started learning different ways to make tofu tasty (I'm honestly not sure I ever succeeded there). She held fast for about nine months. I don't remember exactly what made her call it quits, but I do recall her next diet was pretty much nothing but hamburgers. She seemed to be on a quest to find the best hamburger or cheeseburger known to man; on a road trip once, she declared, quite loudly, that she wanted to "marry

46

this burger" (which meant it was really good, something dad and I figured out when she was much younger and often said she wanted to marry cheese). Last year, she decided to take up the vegetarian habit once again; her motivations seemed to be based more on principle than taste. Given that the rest of us are loud and proud meat-eaters, her principles often fall on deaf ears – particularly the Professor's, who seemed to have declared it his mission to change her mind. But I tried not to let him batter her ideals too much (and I silenced my own Gollum voice as well). The vegetarian lifestyle is not something I'd choose for myself (and I did worry about her not getting enough protein), but I figured as long as she was smart it and happy, who was I to judge? (Though I'll admit to being happy when it turned out to be a phase).

There are times when raising children, though, that we must judge – that is, evaluate the wrong and point toward the right. An example of this is when our kids do something that could hurt themselves or others. Sadly, it happens and no parent, no family, is immune.

When Wonder Boy was a toddler, I often called him a handful and would say God gave me him because I had it so easy with the other two. (Such a negative thing to hear someone say about you, huh? Yeah, see the story about epic failure in rule number 1). I just never could seem to keep up with him, no matter how hard I thought I was trying.

One Friday when he was not quite two years old, all three kids and I arrived at the state fairgrounds to help set up an information table for a weekend event. When we first got out of the van, I realized that neither of the two strollers we owned was in the back. I immediately entered panic mode about Wonder Boy running free. As it turned out him running free was the least of my concerns. After we'd been there for quite some time, I simply had to use the bathroom. Feeling guilty that two fellow mommies had agreed to hawk-duty for the older two, I decided it best to take Wonder Boy with me, thinking at least he'd be confined. Inside the stall, he started touching everything and my panic was rising, along with a good case of germophobia. So, quite proud of myself in my ability to distract him with shiny objects, I pulled my car keys out of my jacket pocket and enticed him away from the garbage can. He jingled and jangled with them and seemed to be having quite the time, and I was pleased that he wasn't crawling on the nasty floor or kissing the stall walls. As I rose from my seated position and pushed the handle to flush, the unthinkable happened. What replays in my mind's eye is a slow-motion shot accompanied by a long and loud "NOOOOOO," though it was really just a split-second. Wonder Boy threw my keys into the spiraling, flushing, emptying toilet bowl. And just like that, the keys were gone, leaving 3 kids (and maybe 1 diaper) stranded at the state fairgrounds with a mom who was on the verge of collapsing into a heaping mess on the floor until dad could arrive (only after rescheduling a meeting he was in the middle of leading) with a spare key. I was panicked, upset, frantic, sick and mad as heck … at my toddler and myself. I was mad at him for something he didn't know was wrong and mad at myself for not seeing it coming.

Because moms expect themselves to be clairvoyant (I clearly hadn't yet evolved to Professor X'hood); and because anger solves things, right? Wrong.

Thankfully, love is stronger than that and keeps no record of wrongs (even when we pesky humans do).

Fortunately, I don't think he had any idea that anything was wrong, since he proceeded to run like crazy around the exhibition hall while we waited. By the time we finally got home that evening, I was able to laugh (perhaps I was just all cried out) and we tried to talk to Wonder Boy about what not to do in the bathroom. Of course, at his age, not much, if anything, sunk in; and thus began the "we don't put things in toilets" phase of his life.

Even though the keys incident may have scarred me a little emotionally, flushing improper things down toilets are a relatively easy (albeit messy) and non-dangerous issue to address. However, I'll never forget when I realized Wonder Boy was a bully. I'd like to say that he became one overnight, but looking back, I had to admit the signs were there. Like the time when he was just learning to walk and he pulled himself up by the collar of a friend … and then pushed that baby down. So I guess I really should have seen this coming – the day he almost got kicked out of daycare. I got a call that the then 3-year-old Wonder Boy was in the daycare director's office and needed to be picked up. When I arrived, I was told that he could not return to school for the rest of the week because he was suspended; the suspension came with a warning that if "something like this" happened again, he'll be asked to leave permanently. "Something like this" referred to his having gone ballistic on his classmates. In the course of one day, Wonder Boy had scratched one kid on the neck, punched another full on in the mouth, and swung yet another around by the shirt collar while the kid cried for his mommy. From what I could gather, two of the three resulted in blood flow. I think I spent most of the next several days crying for my mommy and wondering how to "fix" my toddler. He returned to daycare the next week and, despite his announcement of "I be good!" at pick-up,

I learned he had twisted a child's ear until it turned red (which he delightedly called, "inferno"). Thankfully, the ear-twisting didn't constitute "something like this," so he was allowed to continue attending. I remember vividly thinking that I wouldn't blame the daycare if they ultimately did give him the boot. If the tables had been turned, and my kid was the one being terrorized by another, I might have demanded it.

Despite Wonder Boy being our third child, this situation was a first for us. The Girl was the "bitee" at daycare and was always more likely to cry with someone than be the cause of the crying. The Professor, though he liked to rough-house at home, was a quiet little angel at school. But, as they say, all kids are unique. Wonder Boy's bullish behavior continued much to our dismay. So dad and I tried talking to Wonder Boy ("You shouldn't be mean to the other kids," "Keep your hands to yourself," "You would be sad if someone did that to you, wouldn't you?"). Then we moved on to spanking when he "acted out" at daycare. We tried positive reinforcement (we'd hang his good daily reports on the wall and gush about them); we tried restriction (from toys or TV). We tried flat-out bribery ("I'll buy you an ice cream/toy/the world if you'll just be nice today"). We were at our wit's end by the time Wonder Boy's tenure at daycare came to a close. When he started pre-K and made it through the first week without incident, I thought we'd turned a corner. Silly me. On his 6th day at his new school, I received the following note in his take-home folder:

> "[Wonder Boy] was not making good
> choices today. He would not sit on the
> carpet and chose to roll around on the
> floor and stand on his head. In line for

breakfast, he had a kicking battle with another student. He was running around the cafeteria after lunch and when [the teacher's aide] tried to take his hand and lead him back to our line, he just rolled around on the floor. At naptime, he kept putting his feet on others' posters after being asked to stop."

I got the feeling the note would have continued had the paper been bigger. I'll admit I was a little pleased that there wasn't any violence against other kids, aside from the "kicking battle," which sounded mutual. I was well past thinking Wonder Boy was just "going through a phase" and was ready to pull my hair out. When I spoke with his teacher shortly after receiving the note, she assured me that it was nothing she couldn't handle. I'm pretty sure I looked at her with awe. I was struggling to handle my one "precocious child" when she had 20 to corral.

But she was right. She handled it. By Christmas break of that year, Wonder Boy really had turned that corner I'd been looking forward to. Reports from and conferences with his teacher changed; he listened, he played appropriately, he was nice. And anyone who knows him now, at age 10, would likely find it hard to believe that Wonder Boy was ever a bully. He's one of the kindest, most caring, lovable and funny little boys – he doesn't like for anyone to be upset or left out or get into trouble; he makes friends quite easily and all the neighbor boys flock to him. Thank God for pre-k teachers.

I used to be a semi-feminist. Okay well, maybe I was a full-blown feminist. I mean, I never said anything like "girls are better than boys" or "girls can do anything boys can do, only better" – at least not out loud anyway. I can remember saying a time or two that I wasn't a feminist, I was an equalist. I used to think there was no difference between boys and girls other than their private parts. Then I had kids, and all my "no difference" gibberish went out the window.

The Girl came first; then, just before she turned 2, we had the Professor. Early on we started noticing some strangely innate differences between the two, differences that may or may not be attributed to their gender, but differences nonetheless. Some of the differences did seem gender-specific and I fell into the trap of trying to categorize my kids. Some of the differences were so random and so stark that it was kind of funny. For instance, once they were both on regular table food, cleaning up always revealed the same thing — one plate would be completely devoid of all meat, with pasta left untouched; while the other would have no pasta remaining, but the meat untouched — veggies were always a crap shoot. The Professor would eat any kind of meat you put in front of him but didn't like rice or noodles or potatoes. The Girl loved any kind of pasta but wouldn't eat meat to save her life (funny, I guess we should have seen the whole-vegetarian thing coming).

A big difference between the two had to do with sharing information. The Girl has always told every excruciating detail of exchanges between her and a friend, right down to the ums, while the Professor didn't tell me for 2 months that he was in gifted and talented at school. To this day, the Girl will report on her day, class by class or conversation by conversation, while getting information out of the Professor on the other hand is still a little like pulling teeth; you have to ask direct questions and typically more than one or two to find out everything because he seems to enjoy answering in monosyllables only. But get him one-on-one and in a good mood and he can give his sister a run for her money in the talking department. But then Wonder Boy came along and that boy can put us all to shame. He loves to talk about anything and everything, from video games to feelings, and given his extra-long meal-time prayers ("Thank you God for the farmers who grow the food and the land you gave to them to do it …") might just be talking and ministering to the world one day.

Another difference between the two older ones when they were little was a bit more subtle, evident in the way they played. The Girl always wanted someone to watch her do something or play something with her. The Professor, however, was perfectly happy just to sit and play on his own … he'd occupy himself for hours, adding sound effects to his toy cars and action figures and only coming out of his imagination to ask for juice or a snack. Once Wonder Boy came along and was big enough to play with the same kind of stories, I became convinced that the ability to make sound effects is innate in boy DNA. The way they play, though, is probably indicative of a more significant personality distinction. The Girl is more sensitive to other's feelings, while the Professor is sensitive at times but rarely shows it. He's more concerned with getting a laugh, while she's just more concerned. Wonder Boy seems to be a well-balanced mixture of the two; he loves playing with friends and making people laugh and genuinely wants people to be happy, but also enjoys playing alone at times.

Every child, every person, is unique. God made us to be different. Wouldn't life be so boring otherwise? This seems like a no-brainer, but we parents need the reminder. Even though somewhere deep down, we hate stereotypes, we use things like gender or birth order to identify who are kids are or why they behave the way they do. And not just them. We use the same arbitrariness to define ourselves as parents: like saying you're a #boymom somehow means your life is made up of more dirt and less drama. Trust me, drama – and melodrama and moodiness – is not gender-specific. Neither is dirt for that matter (you should see the Girl's room). The point, though, is that instead of trying to box our children in categories to define who they are, we have to remember Who made them and be thankful for the blessing.

Remembering Who made our children means accepting and appreciating their differences, from each other and from ourselves. Though our kids most definitely pick up traits and habits from us, they are not meant to be our clones. God looked at the world and said it needed my children, and yours too, not just more of us.

While it's safe to say that "bullying" was a phase for Wonder Boy, just like copying others style was for the Girl, there will always be times when I'm not happy with the actions (or even personality traits) of one or more of my children. But, as I hope I've established already, they could probably say the same about me. While I'm called to train them up right and help them avoid (or at least learn from) mistakes, I'm not meant to change them into miniature versions of myself. I'm meant to help them become the best versions of themselves and to love them wholeheartedly in the process.

What a wretched man I am! Who will rescue me from this body of death? Thanks be to God – through Jesus Christ our Lord!

...

Therefore, there is now no condemnation for those who are in Christ Jesus, because through Christ Jesus the law of the Spirit of life set me free from the law of sin and death.
-Romans 7:25-26; 8:1-2 (NIV)

RULE #5: Give it (All) to God

Each stage has its own challenges and own rewards. Sometimes in the day-to-day grind, all we can see are the challenges, often not noticing the rewards until they're missed. When children are very young, they depend on their parents for everything. Let this sink in: as babies, the only thing children can do for themselves is sleep (and they often don't want to). As they age, children gain more and more independence. Independence is a good thing, but we all want to feel needed (whether we readily admit it or not). When kids are younger, they've no problem needing mom. The older they get, kids get embarrassed if they show how they need mom. And all the while, though we age as they do, we're basically the same mom or parent we started out as (mere humans doing the best we can and hopefully learning from our mistakes along the way). Whether going through "phases" or just trying to figure out who they are, our children develop personalities that may or may not reflect our own. It's probably a staple of parenthood that, at some point, in seeing yourself in your kids, you'll empathize with what your parents dealt with in raising you. I may have had a bit of a smart-mouth as a child (but I've clearly grown out of it). There are times when I think the Professor is me made over, and that's not a good thing.

Not long after he turned seven, the Professor picked up a book that had been lying on my nightstand:

Professor: (Sounding out the title) *"Lessons for a Supermom."* (Then, questioning either himself or the book cover) *Lessons for a supermom? Mommy?*

Me: *What?*

Professor: *What is this "Lessons for a supermom"?*

Me: *A book.* (I couldn't help myself. No wonder he's a smart-aleck.)

Professor: (Huffing) *No. I know that. Why do you have it?*

Me. *Someone gave it to me, I think, for a gift.*

Professor: (Clearly contemplating that for a moment) *Have you read it?*

Me: *Nope.*

Professor: *Why not?*

Me: *I don't know; I just haven't had time I guess.*

Professor: *Well ... you should.*

At this point, the Girl shouted his name just as I was saying "I know ... I've got lots to read though ..."

Yep, she got there before me. I looked up to see the hint of a smirk twisted up on his face.

Professor: *You need to read it, so you'll be a supermom* (and he grinned, clearly satisfied with his delivery).

The Girl: (In that exasperated tone she takes with him when attempting to distance herself as the older and wiser of the two) *She already is.*

The whole conversation was yet another taste of the contrast between them. There have been occasions when I suspected manipulation or "brown-nosing" from the Girl, but this was not one of them. No, this was just a classic example of her trying to shield my feelings from what she sensed to be an insensitive attack. From her brother's perspective, though, he saw an opportunity for humor at someone else's expense. Fortunately, I suppose, my feelings have never been as fragile as the Girl assumes. To her, feelings are to be handled with tender loving care, like a snowglobe double-packed in bubble wrap, suspended in Styrofoam and painstakingly preserved to live another day.

The Professor has a history of breaking snowglobes (no, really, just ask the staff at Kroger).

Of course, I'm no supermom, and I'm certainly not implying that here. Parenting is hard, y'all. There's no instruction manual. Every kid is different. Yada, yada, yada. So what do we, as parents, do when something comes up and we feel blindsided or out of our depth? Where do we turn?

To God. Seriously, I don't know how I would have made without faith, without knowing that God is for me … and my kids. (He's for you, too!)

When I was in the thick of my glory days writing this book, parenthood hurled yet another conundrum at Bryan and myself. We've survived raising a toddler who bullied others (seriously, a toddler bully!) and by the grace of God, Wonder Boy is a sweetheart now. We've faced good grades and bad, good friends and bad, and good attitudes and bad. We've seen the effects of peer pressure, from the giving and receiving end, and a multitude of "relationship" issues. We've watched as our children grow and mature, pushing boundaries both real and perceived. We've survived these things because we've given them to God. But God is always listening, and He is always working in your life and the lives of your children.

When the kids have been under attack – in the midst of esteem issues, confused about themselves or the world in general, stressed or anxious about the uncertainty of the future, or just struggling to know who they are – they often respond in one of two ways – the silent treatment or the lash-out. Of course, neither is healthy. Sometimes no matter what you say or do when your child is facing a decision or going through a struggle, the child won't hear you.

And sometimes, he (or she) just needs someone else to listen.

Both of the older two have attended counseling at different times. I saw a therapist regularly when I was in my twenties and have always thought that having someone who will objectively listen to you without judgment is a good thing. While the Girl enjoyed her sessions, the Professor wasn't big on talking about his feelings, particularly to a stranger. Without breaking confidentiality, the counselor told me that some days he would simply sit and say nothing – not a single word – no matter what she tried; he'll tell you he was just emulating Matt Damon in *Good Will Hunting* (it's possible that we watch too many movies).

For the short time we lived in Franklin, Tennessee, we attended an adult Bible study class based on the book, *Shepherding a Child's Heart.* One of the co-leaders often talked quite a bit about her two sons and how they were very different from one another. In a rather moving moment once, she explained how, despite her propensity to try to "toughen up" her oldest son, she truly hoped she never did, because he was "wonderfully made" by God. I was reminded of this yet again just a couple of years ago. Teenagers are often the focus of a lot of negativity from parents. No doubt it's a volatile time in one's life, with so many physical and emotional changes and parents who just don't understand (despite the fact that they all went through it themselves once). (Cue the Fresh Prince, a.k.a. Will Smith, circa 1988). I'm not saying that every day is a piece of cake, but we must remember to acknowledge and embrace the good that can come with our children getting older. For Mother's Day a few years ago, when the Girl was about 13, she cooked breakfast for the family; she had a little help from dad, but it was her idea. They didn't even wake me up until my plate of food, cup of coffee, and gifts (which she wrapped) were waiting at my seat at the table. Then, while dad and I finished our coffee, she summoned her brothers to her room so they could call their grandmother; this without any prompting from either of us. And when dad said they should clean the kitchen, because they shouldn't leave the mess for me to clean, she dutifully worked at whatever was needed (even while her brother complained that he "already did a job").

Now I could have just used this story to say look what I great job I've done as a mother. But anyone who knows me wouldn't let me get away with that. I couldn't even contain my cynicism when I hugged the Girl and told her thanks, adding, "You don't want anything, do ya?" But I am learning to appreciate her more and more and wouldn't want to change her for anything. God gave my Girl the sweetest heart, and I think (I hope) she might be wearing off on me.

Lest you fall back into the trap that the Girl, being a girl, has more sensitive feelings than her brother, consider how often our children identify themselves by what we say about them. This should make you think twice about the way you describe them; I know it's something I'm working on.

Parenting issues are as unique as the children they involve. Nevertheless, the Creator of the Universe hears our every prayer, spoken and unspoken, oral and written, eloquent and blubbering. And when He moves, He MOVES. We just must be willing to see it. I'm not so naïve to think that some other nerve-rattling issue won't pop up tomorrow or even willing to promise that I won't worry about my kids; but I'm confident that God is always in control. He's just waiting for us to seek Him.

We need to love our children for who they are, not who the world says they're supposed to be. These past weeks have reminded me that my children, even when they drive me crazy, are blessings. God entrusted them to me.

But He didn't just say, "Have at it; you're on your own." He's with me every step of the way. Rather than leaning in to Him only when the going gets tough; I should keep Him at the center of every step. He should be on my mind and in my heart not only when I tell my children how much I love them, but also when I'm disciplining or having the tough conversations.

And I need to be sure I tell them how much He loves them too: how His love is infinitely more perfect and true than mine could ever be even though I'm their mother. We don't need to be super-parents; we just need to trust in Him.

And so, finally, I leave you with this truth: the greatest gifts we can give our children, the two things every unique child needs – love and faith.

Of course, a healthy sense of humor can't hurt anything either.

She is clothed with strength and dignity;
She can laugh at the days to come.
-Proverbs 31:25 (NIV)

Epilogue

I've been a writer for as long as I can remember. In fact, I've had several books that I've been "working on" for more than half my life. But I'd never finished a complete draft of one before this book. When I committed to completing this book, it took several days of long hours in front of the computer (quite often to Lauren Daigle's *How Can It Be* as soundtrack). Days that went uninterrupted – no taxiing of kids to or from places, no grocery shopping trips – those days seemed glorious. On one of those glory days, as I was over-the-moon with myself for being so productive, I found my 10-year-old still in his underwear at 4 pm watching TV and eating goldfish. Now the underwear was a non-issue (truth is, he can go from fully-clothed to nothing but briefs like a superhero without the need of a telephone booth); but, as it turned out, those goldfish were all he'd eaten the entire day. Believe me, the irony of me spending so much time working on a "parenting book" while my kid literally fends for himself is not lost on me. But, hey, he really likes goldfish. So I'm sticking to rule #1.

At times as I've put this book together, pulling old stories from my blog and sharing more recent happenings, I've wondered if I'm sharing "too much." A few years ago, I acknowledged that using my kids' lives as "blog fodder," as open books to the world, might be embarrassing and/or an invasion of their privacy. I don't mean privacy as in knowing what's in their rooms or checking their text messages; I've got no problem with that. But I wondered if I should use their lives as material. Blogs (and books) are public and public is forever. The more and more they talk to me about "stuff," I want to encourage open communication and certainly don't want to break confidences or make them feel as though I'm making fun or sharing secrets. So the kids were the first to read this book, agreeing to what they were comfortable with me sharing and giving me the chance to, when directed, protect their privacy. Whether it's surviving on snacks or letting me tell their life stories, my children (and husband) have given me a lot of grace, and I can't thank them enough for the understanding and support.

Acknowledgements and Credits

Thanks to the numerous friends and colleagues who offered to read this book during its various stages of development. A special thanks to those who took time to offer proofreading, editing, feedback and/or encouragement; namely: Tanner Cangelosi, Jayna Coppedge, Pen Fist, Tony Houston, Laura McCoy and Lacey Thacker.

Special thanks to Tanner Cangelosi for designing the cover for this book.

We are a family of nerds, which means our lives (and therefore, the stories in this book) are inundated with a plethora of pop culture and fandom references. Whether it's television shows, movie references, or comic book heroes, etc., this author does not claim any ownership of any those characters or their stories. I'm simply happy for the family entertainment (so, thanks Disney, Marvel, DC, Fox and so on).

Made in the USA
Lexington, KY
27 June 2017